CW00556009

SOLO GUITAR PLAYING

SOLO GUITAR PLAYING

Book 2

by Frederick M. Noad, M.A.

Amsco Publications
New York/London/Paris/Sydney/Madrid/Copenhagen

An audio CD of the complete repertoire pieces contained in *Solo Guitar Book 2*
performed by the author and Ed Flower is available from your local music dealer
or through Amsco Publications: Use Order No. OM 24604. The price is US$12.95.

Copyright © 1977 by Frederick M. Noad

This book published 1999 by Amsco Publications,
A Division of Music Sales Corporation, New York

tenth printing: 1999

All rights reserved. No part of this book may be
reproduced in any form or by any electronic or mechanical means,
including information storage and retrieval systems,
without permission in writing from the publisher.

Order No. AM 949476
US International Standard Book Number: 0.8256.1307.8
UK International Standard Book Number: 0.7119.7655.4.

Exclusive Distributors:
Music Sales Corporation
257 Park Avenue South, New York, NY 10010 USA
Music Sales Limited
8/9 Frith Street, London W1V 5TZ England
Music Sales Pty. Limited
120 Rothschild Street, Rosebery, Sydney, NSW 2018, Australia

Printed in the United States of America by
Vicks Lithograph and Printing Corporation

For Manuel de la Chica of Granada,
good friend and great guitar maker

CONTENTS

PREFACE

THE WIDESPREAD ACCEPTANCE OF Book 1 of *Solo Guitar Playing* has prompted me to continue the course of instruction embodied in it to the next level of both technique and musicianship. This is not to say that Book 2 is a very advanced or complicated manual for the aspiring professional, but rather that it attempts to provide the necessary background and assistance to those who wish to play more interesting repertoire.

Many of the pieces in this volume are not very much more difficult than those in the first volume, but each has been chosen to illustrate a particular point of style, a particular period, or a particular technique. The primary objective is to help the student to play music of intrinsic value with taste and polish, whether that music be technically demanding or of great simplicity.

It is hard to overstress the importance of trying to master one level before moving to another. The methods offered here for the improvement of technique should not be taken as an invitation to approach those compositions of virtuoso level that are so unappealing to the listener when imperfectly played. Such pieces will in time fall naturally within the grasp of some students; but invariably they will be those who have applied themselves with enthusiasm to mastering, in detail, each of the intermediate steps of proficiency.

I have written this book primarily for the amateur, since of the enormous number of people who fall under the spell of the guitar only a handful become professionals, and those not always the best players. Accordingly, I have taken a realistic view of the amount of practice time available to the amateur, and I have made every effort to include exercises of proven effectiveness in producing the maximum result in the minimum time.

Practice time is precious to the amateur musician, whether it be a restorative hour after the working day or a private moment late at night; and even the university music student, because of the demands of academic classes, must often snatch time when he can. In these circumstances it is not realistic to expect all of this time to be given to scales or exercises, yet no progress will be made if the time is limited to the repetition of memorized pieces. A balance has to be found to avoid the well-known "plateau" feeling of arrested progress and to enjoy continued self improvement.

I have chosen the repertoire in this volume with just such a balance in mind. The first passion for the guitar is usually born from hearing romantic music of the type particularly idiomatic to the instrument. (As typical examples one may cite Tárrega's study in tremolo *Recuerdos de la Alhambra* in this volume and the anonymous *Romance* in the first volume. Also the music of J. S. Bach played on the guitar has drawn many not only to the guitar but also to Bach.) But limitations of repertoire necessitate the exploration of other periods and composers, and this in turn requires at least some study of period styles. Baroque music has a spice of its own that is lost if it is played in the style of Mendelssohn, which is equally inappropriate for the lute music of the Renaissance. Because each musical era has almost infinite variety, no one can expect to be a master of all periods; but broadening one's musical viewpoint is as necessary to the guitarist as to the player of any other instrument. Thus, I have chosen the repertoire offered here from a variety of periods, and I have made suggestions for appropriate interpretation of each piece.

Any player who has progressed to the point of studying from this book will be aware that the guitar is not an easy instrument to play well. It has no mechanical devices to assist the player, and most of the time both hands must be employed with minute precision just to produce a single satisfactory note. Those who do not play are usually unaware of this difficulty, and tend to be surprised to see a guitarist struggling to perfect music that sounds as easy as a beginner's piano piece. This is a cross that must be borne by the players of this nonmechanical instrument, a burden I share with great sympathy. But the guitarist's compensation lies in the range of tonal quality and variety impossible for the pianist, in the rich harmony unavailable to the violinist, and in the dynamic range totally beyond the harpsichordist. For all its disadvantages, the guitar offers such sensitivity and range to those who love it that we face a constant challenge to overcome the physical problems and to reveal its particular and highly individual magic.

LESSON ONE
RHYTHM AND COUNTING

IN ORDER TO APPROACH THE MUSIC in this volume without undue difficulty it is necessary to review and improve the basic skills of sight reading and technique. These are the fundamental tools that will facilitate a logical progress through the different topics discussed below.

The conventional methods of counting quarter, eighth, and sixteenth notes are covered in Book 1, but further practice is necessary to build confidence in reading more complex rhythmic figures. Now is the time to realize that the innate sense of rhythm claimed by many students is usually in fact a memory, derived from listening to records or other players, which is of no assistance in the preparation of new music.

The ability to unravel the time of a new piece depends only on developing the habit of counting while playing, and this in turn depends upon going slowly enough to accomplish notes and rhythm together. It helps also to count out the rhythm of a passage *before* starting to play.

DOTTED NOTES

All teachers recognize the dotted note as the first major hurdle in teaching beginners to count. For the purposes of this book we must assume that there is no problem counting the tempos and playing the notes in examples (a) and (b). If there *is* difficulty, the explanation of dotted notes and the accompanying exercises in Book 1 should be thoroughly reviewed.

A Common Baroque Pattern

In the baroque period it was common to use sequences of dotted eighth notes followed by sixteenths, as in example (c).

According to counting rules the basic scheme should be

One - e - and - a Two - e - and - a Three - e - and - a Four - e - and - a

In practice this number of syllables tends to slow down what is usually a faster moving passage. With familiarity, the *e-and* may be eliminated, and the passage counted

One   a Two   a Three   a Four   a

To clarify the point, count example (c) both ways, then play it in tempo.

The Reverse Pattern

When the pattern is reversed as in example (d), the rhythm at first sight seems more complicated.

Applying the counting rules, however, will again expose the basic pattern:

One - e - and - a Two-e-and-a - Three - e - and-a Four - e- and-a

As in example (c) when the relationship is thoroughly understood the counting may be simplified. Here, the simple count would be

One - e   Two - e   Three - e   Four - e

DOUBLE DOTTING

A second dot increases the value of a note by half the value of the previous dot. Thus, if a dot added to a half note increases its value by a quarter (half the value of the original note), a second dot will add the duration of an eighth note:

In example (e) notice that the double-dotted half note extends into the fourth beat, which must therefore be counted before the following note is played.

Double-Dotted Quarter Notes

The second dot adds the duration of a sixteenth note to a dotted quarter note, simply solved by using the *One-e-and-a* breakdown:

In practice a simpler count is used:

One   Two a Three   Four a One

The *aThree* is counted as if it were a single word, thereby giving the characteristic "skip" feeling of the sixteenth that normally follows the double-dotted quarter. Try to feel this while counting and playing example (f).

Double-Dotted Eighth Notes

It will be apparent from the previous section that the use of double dots has the effect of "spiking" the rhythm. In the baroque period, composers often used double dotting in pieces involving long sequences of dotted eighths followed by sixteenths to add liveliness and sparkle to the conventional pattern. And it was not uncommon for players to improvise double dotting where the score contained only single dots.

The relationship of the double-dotted eighth to the thirty-second note that usually follows is the same as that of the double-dotted quarter to the following sixteenth. Thus, in common time the pattern may be found by using the system explained in the previous section, but counting eight (eighth-note) beats to the bar instead of four (quarter-note) beats. In practice, the following simplified (if seemingly inexact) method may be used.

First, with a regular beat, and saying each of the *a* sounds as rapidly as possible, count aloud: "One, aTwo, aThree, aFour." If the *a* sound falls just fractionally before the downbeat, the rhythm will be very close to that of example (g).

One   a Two   a Three   a Four

PRACTICAL EXERCISES

In the following four exercises the student is recommended to count out at least one full line before commencing to play. As in all the duet exercises in this book, the upper staff is for the student and the lower for the teacher.

Exercise 1

Exercise 2

Exercise 3

(Theme by Vivaldi)

Exercise 4

(Theme by Handel)

LESSON TWO
SCALE TECHNIQUE

PROBABLY MORE HAS BEEN WRITTEN AND SAID about scales than any other aspect of technique, and traditionally the rote learning and repetition of scales in all keys has been considered a fundamental instruction device for all instruments. In the introduction to his scale book,* Andrés Segovia recommends that the aspiring player devote two hours a day to scales; this advice from such an authority is treated with great reverence by serious students, although few of them actually follow it. The simple fact is that of the vast number of people interested in improving their ability only a few have that much time each day to give to one aspect of technique.

It is curious to note that the guitar repertoire in general contains few extended scales in comparison with the music for almost any other instrument. Certainly the *Concierto de Aranjuez* has many, but according to the composer the scales were included to give a feeling of flamenco. However the works of, for instance, Fernando Sor contain only a very occasional scale of as much as an octave in length.

Nevertheless, those who can play scales well like to show them off, and there is no surer way to capture an audience than with a dazzling display of fast passages of this kind. As a result the few pieces that demand excellent scale work appear again and again on concert programs.

For the amateur it seems to me that some reasonable compromise must be reached. With only an hour or two available for practice the time allotted to scales must be in proportion to their overall importance, and certainly an honest fifteen minutes daily will achieve more than an occasional, compulsive two-hour assault.

TONE QUALITY

The pracitce of scales furnishes the opportunity to work in detail on the most fundamental of techniques, the simple alternation of the fingers. The precise angle of attack of the nails may be checked for optimum tone quality, and the touch may be adjusted to ensure complete evenness of volume and quality from one note to another. For this type of detailed and analytical work the slow scale is almost the perfect vehicle.

* Andrés Segovia, ed., *Diatonic Major and Minor Scales* (Washington, D.C.: Columbia Music Co., 1953).

RIGHT-HAND STABILITY

In past centuries it was customary for players to support the right hand in a fixed position by resting the little finger on the soundboard near the bridge. Modern technique has abandoned this position as being too restrictive, but the necessity remains of a stable position for the right hand from which the various techniques can be accomplished without excessive movement. For instance, when playing a descending scale that travels from the first string to the sixth there is a natural tendency to pull the hand back toward the sixth string and away from the central position of stability. This is also associated with the bad habit of using a movement of the whole hand to play a note instead of just the finger moving from the knuckle.

REST AND FREE STROKES

In this book the term "rest stroke" is used when the right-hand finger completes its movement by coming to rest on the adjacent lower string; "free stroke" is used when the finger just clears the adjacent string. These basic movements are fully explained in Book 1, to which reference should be made if the distinction is in any way unclear.

In playing scales, students should practice the free stroke as well as the rest stroke, and there is also value to the mixed scale where free strokes are used for the bass strings, rest strokes for the trebles. In this kind of scale the right hand is more likely to maintain a good position, and the technique corresponds more closely to practical usage in performance, where the use of the rest stroke is a comparative rarity on strings lower than the third.

To summarize, the value of scale practice lies not in just playing the notes but in *how* they are played. The scale is a most useful vehicle for the detailed improvement of basic techniques.

PRACTICAL EXERCISES

The following exercises are based on the simple scale of C major. The principles they demonstrate can, of course, be applied to other scales, for which the recommended text is the Segovia scale book mentioned above.

The scale in exercise 5 should first be memorized thoroughly by playing it with each of the following combinations of fingers, using the rest stroke first, then the free stroke:

1. *i m i m*	3. *i a i a*	5. *a m a m*
2. *m i m i*	4. *a i a i*	6. *m a m a*

Exercise 5

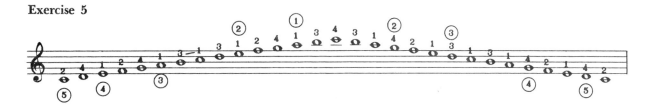

Next, a combination of three fingers may be used as shown in exercise 6. This combination fingering is particularly useful when time is short as a means of warming up each of the right-hand fingers.

Exercise 6

The logic behind this pattern can be applied to all other scales and is based on the following general rules:

1. When three successive notes are played on the same string, the order of fingers is *a, m, i.*
2. When going up the scale, if there are two notes on a string, or two notes followed by a change of position, then these two are played in the order *m, i.*
3. When going down the scale the two-note groups are played *a, i,* rather than *m, i,* when the latter would produce the awkward string crossing of *i* on one string followed by *m* on the next lower. In these circumstances *i* to *a* is more natural.

Exercise 7

As discussed above, the scale in exercise 7 shows a practical balance of rest and free strokes and should be played with the least possible movement of the right hand.

INCREASING SPEED

One of the most effective methods of increasing speed involves the use of dotted notes. Analyzing what occurs, each pair of notes is individually practiced at a higher speed before the faster tempo is applied to all the notes. Practice first the two-note pattern shown in exercise 8. Then practice the opposite combination shown in exercise 9. Finally, practice the complete scale at the higher tempo of exercise 10.

Exercise 8

Exercise 9

Exercise 10

USE OF THE METRONOME

The metronome, a clockwork device invented by Johannes Maelzel (1772–1838), can be used to avoid boredom when working on increased speed and also as a means of measuring progress. The following method has been found to be particularly effective.

1. Choose a moderate speed setting at which the scale can be played smoothly and with evenly matched tonal quality.
2. Move the speed setting to two points faster. Do your best at this tempo even if the result is less than perfect.
3. Move the speed setting *back* one point. At this slower speed practice for perfection again. Overall you will have gained one speed point, and if complete smoothness has been achieved you may continue by again attempting two points faster, then back one again.

The marking "M.M. ♩ = 100" at the head of a piece indicates that the quarter-note beat is to be taken at the setting of 100 beats to a minute. In modern scores the abbreviation "M.M." (Maelzel's Metronome) is often omitted, as in this book, since virtually all metronomes, including electric types, follow the same numbering system.

Note that the click of the metronome marks the beat rather than a particular note value. Thus, in 3/2 time, which is counted in half notes, the beats-per-minute rate will also be given for the half note, e.g., ♩ = 50. In compound time such as 6/8 the beat may be indicated for a triplet, e.g., ♪ = 50, where a click for each eighth note would be inconveniently fast.

VARIED PRACTICE PATTERNS

Common sequences can profitably be practiced using the same basic scale. That shown in exercise 11 is particularly useful, representing a formula frequently encountered in music from the lute era. Other useful exercises can be created around commonplace patterns, such as those shown in examples (a) and (b).

Exercise 11

Exercise 12

Exercise 13

LESSON THREE
SIGHT READING, FRETS 6-8

FOR CONTINUED PROGRESS ON THE GUITAR it is obviously essential to become thoroughly familiar with the higher positions of the fingerboard. A student of the piano will know the location of all the notes on his instrument within a few days; unfortunately, guitar students tend to put off, sometimes for years, the task of mastering the notes of the higher frets. This subject is dealt with in Book 1, but experience has shown that further work is necessary to achieve a comfortable familiarity in this area.

The most effective way to learn the notes within a reasonable time is to combine theory and practice so that what is learned intellectually is immediately reinforced by practical work. The exercises that follow will help build a foundation, but this foundation should be extended and consolidated by further reading, preferably on a daily basis. A few minutes given to sight-reading new material each day will produce truly amazing results in a year.

It is assumed that the student by now knows the notes up to the fifth fret and that he has some knowledge of the higher positions. The position is always identified by the location of the first finger, and includes the next three frets within reach of the second, third, and fourth fingers. Thus the fifth position covers frets 5-8, the sixth position frets 6-9, and so on.

As a first step, review the notes of the sixth fret, then try exercise 14. You will notice that each less familiar note is related in the exercise to a familiar one in a lower position. The recognition of these links is an important step in mastering the fingerboard. After playing exercise 14 a few times, repeat it from memory, naming the notes as they are played. As a final step, name the notes giving the sharp equivalents for flat notes; e.g. say "A sharp" instead of "B flat," "C sharp" instead of "D flat."

Exercise 14

Following the same principle, exercises 15 and 16 relate the notes of the seventh and eighth frets to their lower-position equivalents, and they should receive the same systematic attention.

Exercise 15

Exercise 16

MEMORIZATION EXERCISES

Now here are some further exercises for practice and to test your memorization. In exercises 17–20, use the positions indicated for each. If undue
difficulty is encountered, return to and review exercises 14–16, which are
designed to help you in learning notes.

Exercise 17 Use the third position throughout, barring only where indicated.

Exercise 18   Use the fourth position throughout.

Exercise 19 Use the fifth position throughout.

(Theme by Mozart)

Exercise 20   Use the fifth position except where indicated.

(Theme by Lully)

Exercise 21

(Theme by Sanz)

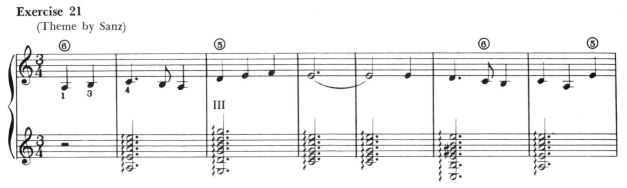

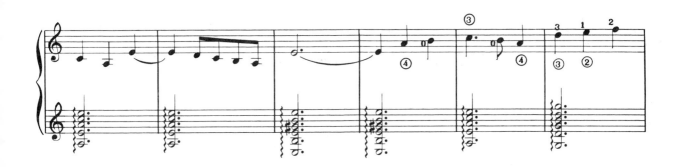

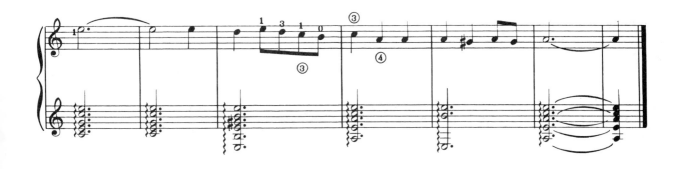

FOUR PIECES WITH STUDY NOTES

STUDY NOTES FOR *PRELUDE*
by Santiago de Murcia

This prelude and the allegro that follows, both published in 1732, are among the last pieces written for the baroque guitar before its decline.

A Do not try to hold the first finger on after the B. This makes the playing of the following F more comfortable.

B The trills may be ignored at this time but should be added after studying the examples in lesson nine.

C The triplet needs practice so that the sound is clear and in accurate time.

D A good rest stroke on the high D will help it to sustain.

E Although both are possible, the full bar will be found more practical than the half bar in this situation.

PRELUDE

Santiago de Murcia (fl. early 1700s)

Andantino (♩ = 84)

STUDY NOTES FOR *ALLEGRO*
by Santiago de Murcia

This piece presents few technical difficulties, but it is important to play it up to tempo to provide a strong contrast to the preceding prelude. The term "allegro" implies cheerfulness as well as speed.

[A]   The complete A chord should be placed at the beginning of the measure. The first finger is flattened to cover both the A and the E, a common and useful fingering since the third and fourth fingers remain free.

[B]   A typical baroque clash. The C sharp forms a dissonance that is quickly resolved by moving to the unison D. The sixth string is more practical than the fifth for the C sharp to avoid inadvertent damping of the open D.

ALLEGRO   Santiago de Murcia (fl. early 1700s)

STUDY NOTES FOR
ANDANTINO ALLA SICILIANA
by Mauro Giuliani

The term "Siciliana" in the title of this piece indicates a gentle, moderate tempo in pastoral style. It presents few technical difficulties and is included here mainly to provide practice in counting dotted and double-dotted notes.

A   The grace notes (small notes) should be executed with a quick pull-off to the main note. (See lesson seven.)

B   The bass below the sixteenth notes can only be imagined, since it is quite impossible to sustain the chord as writtern. Such incongruities occur from time to time in the scores of this period.

C   A practice spot. If the third finger is properly placed on the G it should not be too hard to stretch to a half bar for the A and C sharp. In Giuliani's time the fingerboard was shorter and the stretch consequently easier.

D   The transition to the half bar is easier if the first finger takes the bar position on the G sharp, then slides up covering three strings.

ANDANTINO ALLA SICILIANA   Mauro Giuliani (1781–1829)

STUDY NOTES FOR *ANDANTINO*
by Fernando Sor

Although more of a technical challenge than the previous pieces, this andantino is often performed in concert and has been recorded by Segovia and others; it is thus worth the work involved in preparing it. Careful attention to the left hand when changing position and extra practice for the more difficult chord changes should solve most of the technical problems.

A | This passage could be taken in the fifth position, but the move to the third position then presents a problem. On the whole it seems better as written, although some stretching is required.

B | The fourth, third, and second fingers must be closely tucked in together, as when playing an A major chord in the first position.

C | Because the fourth finger must jump from the first to the second string the chord change here should receive extra practice.

ANDANTINO, Op. 2 No. 3   Fernando Sor (1778–1839)

LESSON FOUR
ARPEGGIOS

THE VARIOUS FORMS OF BROKEN CHORDS known as arpeggios represent an important aspect of right-hand technique. When practiced as exercises they serve to develop a balanced and even touch in the fingers of the right hand, particularly with regard to the problematic *a* (ring) finger.

HISTORICAL IMPORTANCE

In the music of the late Renaissance it was common for guitarists and lutenists to play chords in slightly arpeggiated form, with the fingers following quickly one after another to give a rippling sound—the same effect achieved by playing a chord with a single stroke of the thumb. So common was this practice that it became customary to mark in the music only where this was *not* to be done, i.e., where the chord was to be played as a single sound.

Style Brisé

The technique developed in the baroque period into a new style of playing, in which the harmony was largely broken up into rhythmic arpeggios. Known as the *style brisé* (broken style), this innovation of plucking the strings had a profound influence on music in general, particularly that composed for the keyboard. The change in approach from block harmony to broken style may be clearly heard by playing the following simple examples. In example (a) the cadence is in conventional style; in example (b) the harmony is the same but the cadence is in arpeggio form.

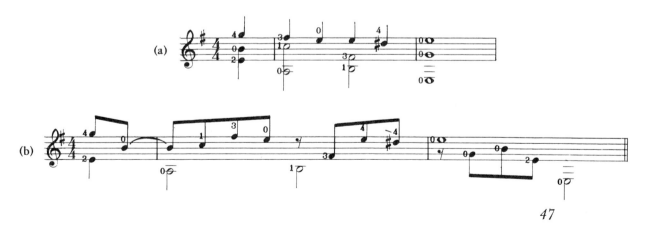

Alberti Bass

The use of the constantly repeated arpeggio in music dates from the early part of the eighteenth century; a simple bass of this kind supporting a melody is known familiarly as an Alberti bass after the composer Domenico Alberti (c. 1710–1740). As a formula it was popular with the early classical guitarists of the nineteenth century and was used by many composers. Giuliani, for one, used it in the opening of his *Divertissement,* opus 78, shown in example (c). Since that period the arpeggio has developed as a particularly idiomatic and appropriate technique for the guitar, forming the basis for some of the most attractive pieces in the repertoire.

(c)

ARPEGGIO TECHNIQUE

Although the primary technique of the arpeggio involves the use of the free stroke, rest strokes are often used where a single note of the arpeggio represents the melody. The distinction can be easily seen in the two examples that follow.

(d)
(e)

In example (d) the arpeggio serves a primarily harmonic function, and the preferred technique would be to use free strokes throughout. The same, of course, would apply if it were the accompaniment to a song.

In example (e) the up-stemmed notes of the triplet groups form part of a melody, and for these notes the rest stroke may be used. However, this is an option rather than a rule; what is needed is a slight emphasis of the melody notes, which can also be achieved by a stronger free stroke. In general it is best to practice this type of passage both ways and to use the technique that seems better to match the mood and tempo of the piece at hand.

THE TARREGA RULES

It is appropriate to restate here the two rules of placement attributed to Francisco Tárrega, since these are rarely fully understood by amateurs.

The first rule relates to the upward-moving arpeggio:

It states that *before* playing the arpeggio, *p, i, m,* and *a* are placed on the strings as if to play a chord. Then when the thumb plays the C, the *i, m,* and *a* fingers remain in position awaiting their turn to play. When *i* plays, the *m* and *a* fingers remain; when *m* plays, the *a* finger remains until it plays the final E. In practice, when there is a fast succession of arpeggios the *i, m,* and *a* fingers will tend to find their places *as* the thumb is playing rather than before it plays. The advantage of playing upward-moving arpeggios this way is that the right hand gains security and accuracy by having the notes prepared in advance.

The second rule applies to arpeggios that, after the thumb stroke, move in a downward direction:

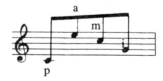

It states that only the outside fingers should be placed on the strings in advance, in this case *p* and *a*.

The purpose of both the Tárrega rules is the same: to increase security by a degree of advance preparation. However, for reverse, or downward-moving arpeggios, the placement of *all* the fingers is considered unnecessarily cumbersome.

GIULIANI'S EXERCISES FOR THE RIGHT HAND

The collection of exercises that follows is from opus 1 of Mauro Giuliani and is still considered a standard work today. The original fingerings are given, but enterprising students will find logical alternatives and will probably wish also to vary the chords.

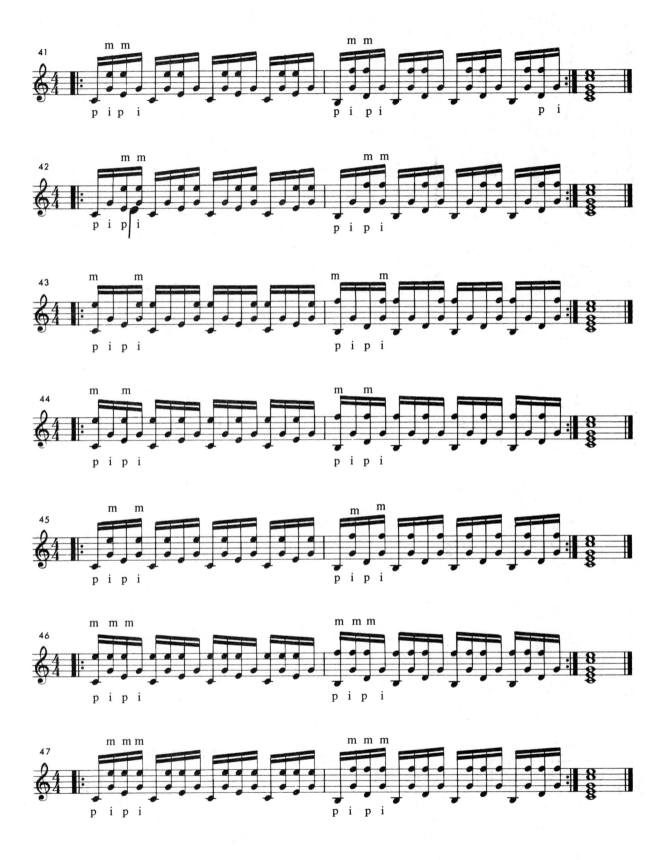

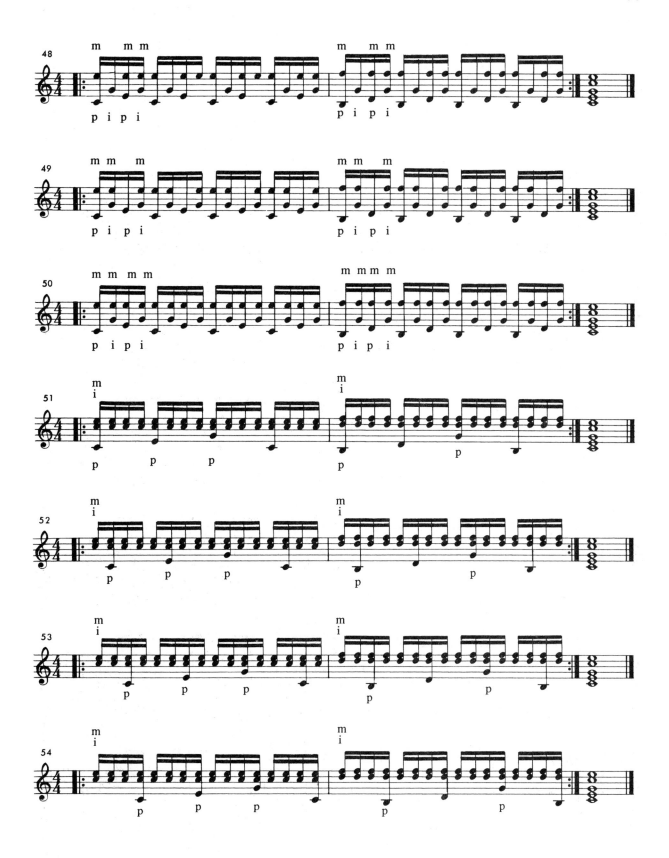

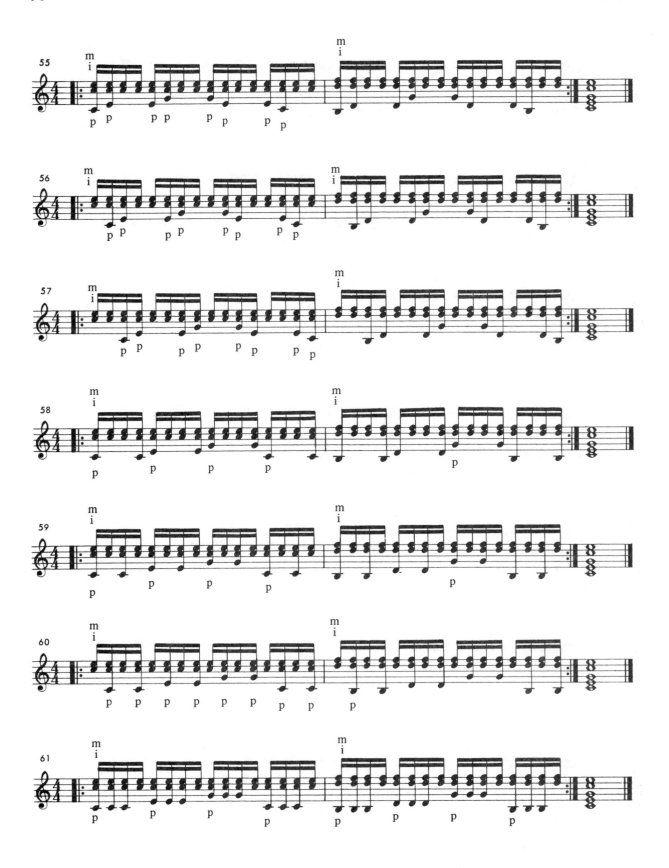

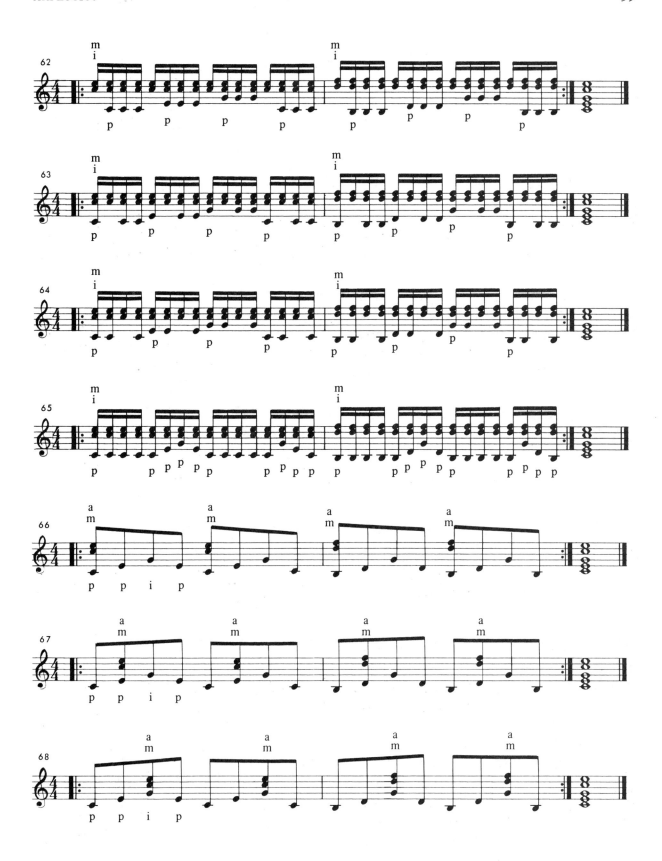

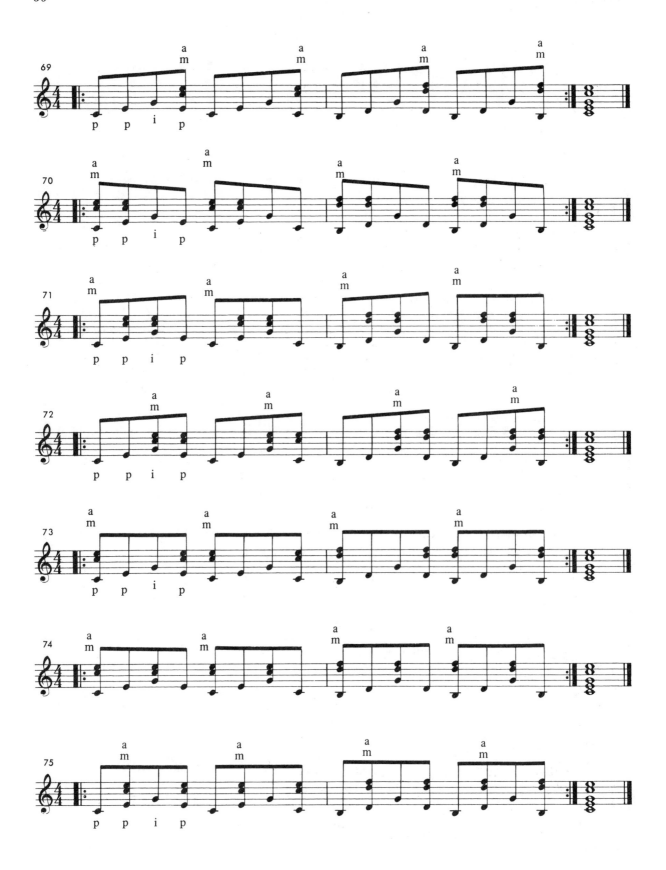

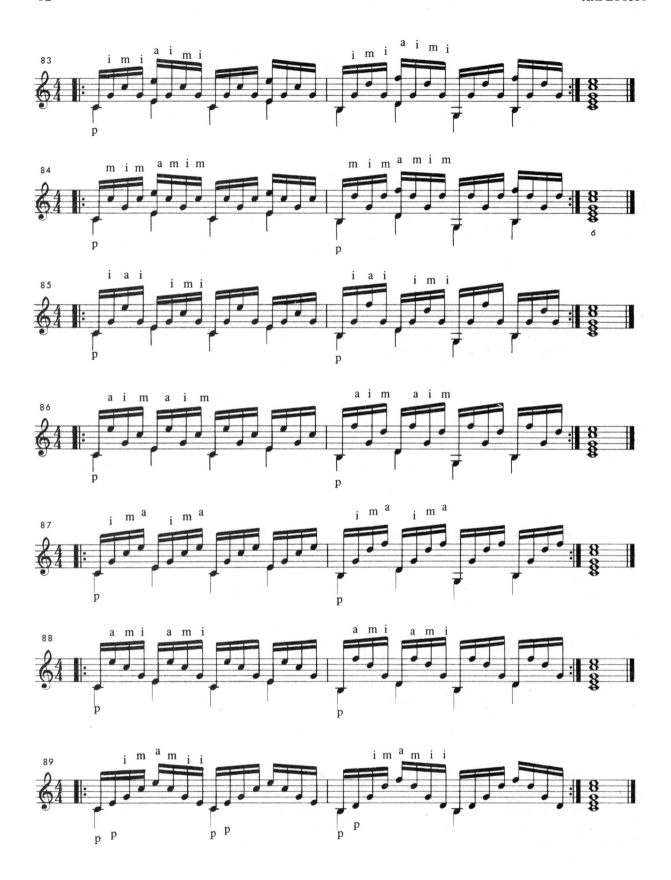

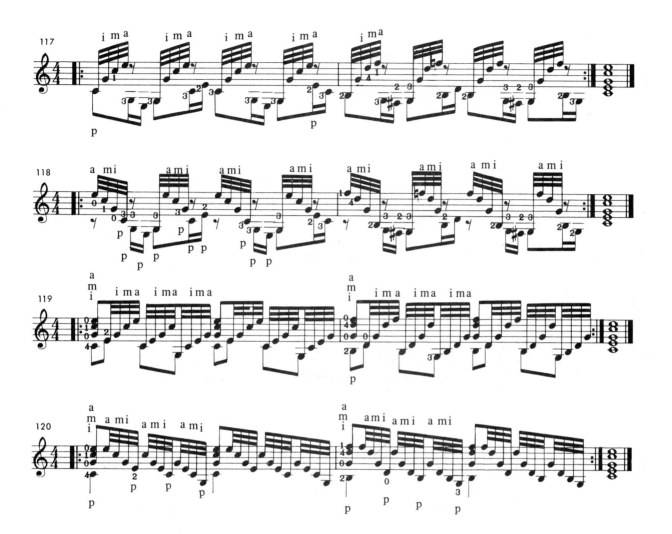

VARIATION ON LA FOLIA

François de Fossa (fl. early 1800s)

FOUR PIECES WITH STUDY NOTES

STUDY NOTES FOR
VARIATION ON LA FOLIA
by François de Fossa

The particular charm of this simple arpeggio study (published in 1820) is due to the alteration of open with stopped strings. The resulting overring is intentional—the style is known as *campanelas* (bell chimes) —and no attempt should be made to damp the notes.

[A] The fourth finger has to move as smoothly as possible from the fourth to the fifth string. Obviously to maintain the tempo it is necessary to lift the fourth-string C a moment before its full quarter-note duration.

STUDY NOTES FOR *VARIATION*
by Fernando Sor

This extract from Sor's *Theme and Variations,* opus 15, serves as a useful study in more extended arpeggios. Once the fingering has been worked out and the piece memorized I suggest working the speed up to the maximum possible consistent with complete accuracy.

[A] After placing the third finger, leave it on, as the same note is needed in the next measure. Besides easing the fingering, this helps to steady the hand.

[B] Do not try to hold the high G; the fourth finger is needed for the low C.

VARIATION, Op. 15 No. 4　　　　　　　　　　Fernando Sor (1778–1839)

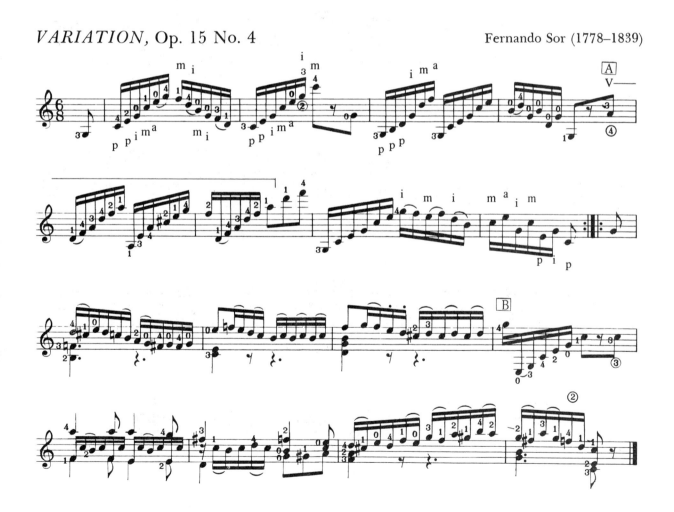

STUDY NOTES FOR *PRELUDE IN D*
by J. S. Bach

This prelude from Bach's first sonata for unaccompanied violoncello, which has long been a favorite with guitarists, affords an attractive vehicle for practicing arpeggios with even, full tone quality. A prelude allows considerable latitude of tempo; the metronome marking given here is my personal preference.

[A] Use a rest stroke on the D sharp to bring out the upper voice. Ideally the D sharp would sustain, but this requires complexities of fingering that are more likely to interrupt the flow of the piece.

[B] This is a curious fingering, but not difficult if the second finger remains fixed on the A and the first finger passes behind it to play the C sharp.

[C] For this measure and the next three the melody is carried by the third string to maintain an even quality of tone.

[D] The chromatic upward scale should build with a gradual crescendo to the high D, which should be played with a rest stroke to bring out a clear, bell-like tone.

PRELUDE IN D

J. S. Bach (1685–1750)

STUDY NOTES FOR *STUDY NO. 1*
by Frederic Hand

This charming study by guitarist Frederic Hand
(recorded by the composer on Hamreem Record
HRS7702) introduces a more contemporary sound
and the somewhat unusual time signature of 5/8.
The composer's specific markings for accents and
for the rest stroke, shown as a small triangle (▽),
help to clarify the required stress.

[A] A certain extension of the hand is necessary
here, but with practice the passage becomes
quite simple.

[B] To perform the glissando, usually abbreviated
as *gliss,* the fourth finger maintains the pressure on the string as the hand moves down
toward the G. This means that the intervening B flat and A are momentarily sounded,
but the movement must be smooth so as not
to interrupt the rhythm.

STUDY NO. 1   Frederic Hand (b. 1947)

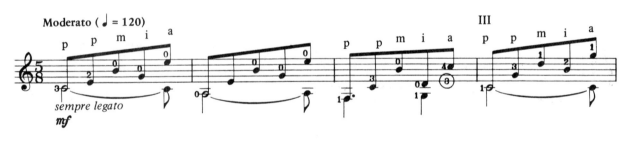

© 1977 by Frederic Hand. All rights reserved. Used by permission.

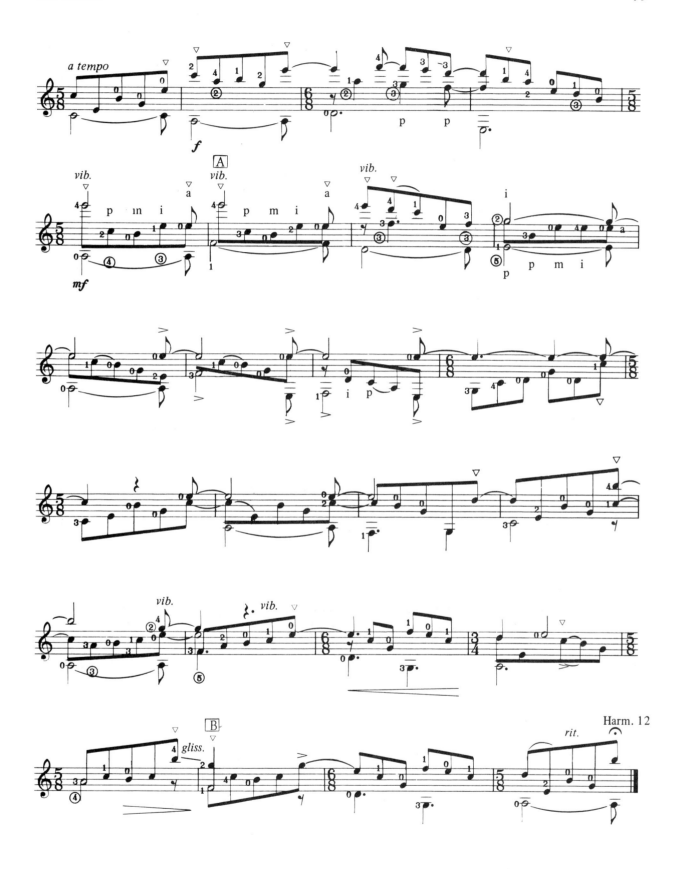

LESSON FIVE
IMPROVING SLUR TECHNIQUE

PRACTICE GIVEN TO THE IMPROVEMENT of slurs (ligados) serves an important dual purpose. First, this form of practice is probably the most effective of all in strengthening the left hand; second, it adds a clarity and definition to overall performance that is the mark of an accomplished player. On the other hand, poorly executed slurs give an untidy and incomplete final result, and the frustrated amateur often is unaware of the reason.

The most simple and basic slur exercises are probably the most effective, and for variety many patterns can easily be devised. The all-important point is *how* the exercises are done. The checklists that follow itemize the main points to watch.

ASCENDING LIGADOS

1. Play the first note clearly and with volume, preferably using a rest stroke.
2. Hammer the second note strongly to achieve a balance with the first. Remember that the hammering finger does not sweep down from a distance but is poised a mere half inch or so above the string before hammering.
3. Be particularly careful not to hurry the tempo by hammering too soon. The finger that hammers must wait until the first note has lasted its correct duration. Try to observe the exact time values as if the two notes were not slurred.

DESCENDING LIGADOS

1. As with the ascending slur, play the first note clearly and with good volume.
2. Remember to pull down with the left-hand finger to sound the second note. At the completion of the movement the finger should be touching the adjacent string, except of course when the slur is on the first string. In a correctly executed slur the pulling finger will also lightly touch the fingerboard after the pull.

3. When playing slurs on the first string be careful to maintain a good left-hand position. There is a strong natural tendency to turn the left hand when making the slur, resulting in a loss of position and consequent insecurity. This is perhaps best illustrated with an example:

In performing the slur from A to G sharp there is some tendency to turn the left hand counterclockwise. The tendency is much greater in playing the slur from B to A. Remember that the *finger* performs the movement, not the whole hand.

EXERCISES FOR DAILY PRACTICE

Some conventional practice patterns are offered below for daily practice. In playing them tend to exaggerate the movements at first, giving an extra strong hammer and pulling off with vigor. Then work toward overall smoothness while still maintaining clarity.

For simplicity the patterns are written in first or second position, working progressively up the string. They may be continued up to the twelfth fret, then back down again. Once they have been memorized, there is an advantage to starting the exercises in the high position and working back down the string, since the closer spacing makes the higher frets somewhat easier in terms of stretch.

Exercise 22

Exercise 23

Exercise 24

Exercise 25

Exercise 26

Exercise 27

Exercise 28

Exercise 29

Exercise 30

Exercise 31

Exercise 32

Exercise 33

THE DOUBLE SLUR

Occasionally a composer will call for the slurring of two notes at once. The principle of execution is exactly the same, but for the descending slur all four left-hand fingers must be prepared in advance.

In example (a) the first and second fingers must be firmly placed on the A and F sharp at the time when the upper chord is played. This is an awkward fingering but necessary for this situation. Then the third and fourth fingers pull in the conventional manner to make the slur. To execute example (b) the first and second fingers are placed on the A and F sharp. After the chord is played the third and fourth fingers hammer simultaneously.

In the nineteenth century a slur sign was sometimes used when the real intention was for a slide. In example (c), from Sor's opus 1, a slide of the first and second fingers would be a more practical solution than attempting a double hammer. A modern score would express the intention more accurately, as in example (d).

It is clear in example (d) that only the first chord is played by the right hand and that the second is sounded by the left-hand fingers sliding with positive motion up to the next fret. This technique can be used in both ascending and descending movements.

THREE PIECES WITH STUDY NOTES

STUDY NOTES FOR *VARIATION*
by Mauro Giuliani

This variation from Giuliani's opus 38 serves as the basis for a study in slurs. After a clear and accurate picture has been formed of the piece, I suggest continued practice to increase your speed to the maximum possible.

[A] The double sharp raises the F two half steps, so that it is the same note as the G natural.

[B] Care should be taken not to pull the hand away from the fingerboard when executing the slurs on the first string. In addition the repeated slides of the third finger must be precise and quick enough to avoid intervening sounds.

VARIATION, from Op. 38   Mauro Giuliani (1781–1829)

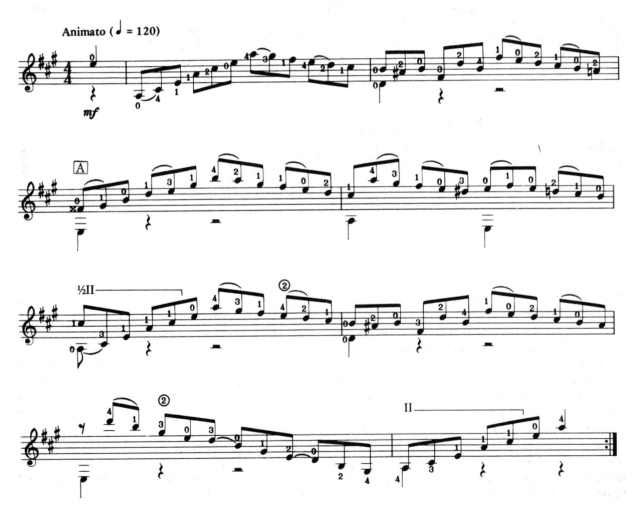

STUDY NOTES FOR *ETUDE*
by Antonio Cano

Trained originally as a surgeon, Antonio Cano later abandoned the scalpel in favor of the guitar and became much celebrated as a professional performer and teacher. His decision to adopt a musical career was influenced by the celebrated guitarist Dionisio Aguado, who was persuaded to attend a recital given by Cano in Madrid in 1847. Following the general and enthusiastic applause for this performance Aguado warmly encouraged him to continue as a guitarist, as a result of which Cano

shortly afterward undertook an extensive concert tour of the principal cities of Spain. This was followed by successful tours of Spain and Portugal that firmly established his celebrity as a performer.

In addition to collections of waltzes and other small compositions, Cano's works include a number of extended operatic fantasies and a method, published in Madrid in 1852, with an interesting accompanying treatise on harmony as applied to the guitar.

This étude, extracted from the method, provides an attractive vehicle for practicing slurs and contains no special technical difficulties.

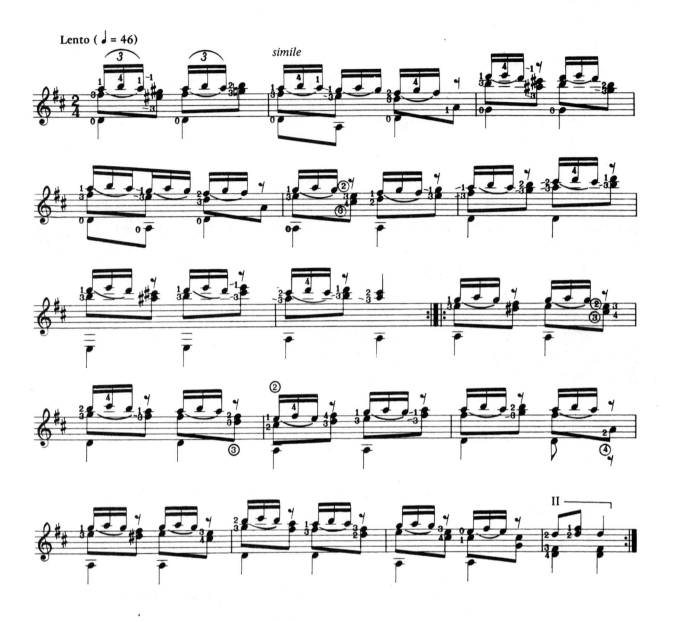

STUDY NOTES FOR *MINUET*
by Fernando Sor

Of the many attractive minuets by Sor this is my personal favorite. It is easy to play, with the exception of two short passages that need extra practice.

A Sor's single-slur indication must obviously be taken as a double slur, performed in this case

by means of a slide. Some force must be used so that the A and F sharp will sound.

B The principal difficulty of the piece lies in this run in thirds. Precise movements and extra practice will remove the difficulty here.

C For an explanation of how to play the turn (∾), see lesson seven. When playing it do not try to sustain the open E, which would be virtually impossible, anyway.

MINUET, Op. 11 No. 5

Fernando Sor (1778–1839)

LESSON SIX
SIGHT READING, FRETS 9–12

THIS LESSON ON SIGHT READING REPRESENTS the completion of the commonly used part of the fingerboard. Particular attention should be paid to the notes on the lower three strings. Because they are less commonly used, they often remain vague in the minds of otherwise proficient amateurs.

Exercises 34, 35, and 36 relate the notes of the ninth, tenth, and eleventh frets to their equivalents in lower positions. The twelfth fret should present no difficulty, since the notes are the octaves of the open strings. As before, repeat each exercise after learning it, saying the notes from memory and, finally, converting the flat notes to their sharp equivalents. In exercises 34 and 36 the notes are expressed as sharps, since sharp keys are more common on the guitar, but remember to repeat from memory the flat equivalents.

MEMORIZATION EXERCISES

The exercises that follow should be played entirely in the indicated position, except where marked. The assistance of fingering is purposely omitted to increase the value of the exercises for note learning.

Exercise 34   (fret 9)

Exercise 35   (fret 10)

Exercise 36   (fret 11)

Exercise 37   (seventh position)

(Theme by Hook)

Exercise 38   (eighth position)

(Theme by de Visée)

Exercise 39 (ninth position)

(Folk Theme)

Exercise 40   (ninth position)

(Theme by Albinoni)

Exercise 41 (eighth and ninth positions)

STUDY NOTES FOR *PRELUDE*
by Francisco Tárrega

In spite of its apparent complexity this prelude is, in fact, easy to play. The reason it is not heard more often—even though it is one of Tárrega's best—is that amateurs have tended to lack the perseverance necessary to sort out the notes in the various positions. It is an excellent test of knowledge of the fingerboard and should not be ignored by the serious student.

The sliding grace notes may be omitted until lessen seven has been studied.

A At this point remember to cover five strings with the half bar in preparation for the low B.

PRELUDE

Francisco Tárrega (1852–1909)

94

LESSON SEVEN
STYLE AND ORNAMENT: CLASSICAL AND ROMANTIC PERIODS

THE MUSIC PLAYED BY GUITARISTS is often classified for reference into five main periods. In each of these the style and flavor of the music is distinct, representing changes in popular taste and evolutionary trends in the technique of composition.

Approximate dates for the reference periods are given below, but of course styles overlapped as one period gradually replaced another. For the purposes of this book, they are considered as follows:

The Late Renaissance	1500–1610
The Baroque Period	1610–1750
The Classical Period	1750–1820
The Romantic Period	1820–1900
The Contemporary Period	1900–

In the particular case of the guitar it is perhaps simpler to consider the nineteenth century, embracing both classical and romantic music, as a single period. The reason is that the second half of the eighteenth century, representing the bulk of the classical period, was one of decline for the guitar. The so-called baroque guitar, with its five pairs of strings, had all but disappeared and had been replaced in favor by the cittern, a wire-strung instrument, similar to a flat-backed mandolin, normally played with a plectrum. This instrument was popularly known as the "English guitar" and was often referred to simply as "the guitar," perhaps because it had taken the place in amateur music formerly occupied by the true guitar.

The beginning of the nineteenth century, however, saw the revival of the guitar, now with six strings, as an instrument of great popularity among both amateurs and professionals. Dominated by the figures of Fernando Sor (1778–1839), Mauro Giuliani (1781–1829), and Ferdinando Carulli (1770–1841), guitar music once again flourished. Elaborate ornamentation was not a characteristic of the period, and in the guitar scores of the first half of the century it is rare to find any indication more elaborate than those for grace notes, turns, or trills.

REFORMED NOTATION

Both Sor and Giuliani were pioneers in the improvement of the form of notation of guitar music, which in its early stage resembled violin music. The two examples below show the original and the "reformed" notation. In example (a), from Carulli's *Sonata,* opus 21, both the chords and the melody are treated as a single part, and the duration of the bass notes is unclear. In example (b), from Sor's *Waltz,* opus 1, the use of upward and downward stems separates the parts and leaves no ambiguity about the duration of the bass notes. This has become the standard form of guitar notation.

Early Guitar Notation

Reformed Notation

GRACE NOTES

These ornaments are indicated by a small note drawn adjacent to a main note, sometimes with a slur joining the two. Whether or not the slur is indicated this technique is invariably used. The grace note is played so quickly as to have no significant time value of its own. In some guitar scores, the small note has an apparent value faster than the main note, but there is little consistency in the values given and the intention was invariably for a fast note whose actual value was borrowed from the main note and not separately counted.

It is particularly important to note that although the grace note is drawn before the beat it was in fact played *on* the beat slightly delaying the main note. Thus in example (c), from Sor's opus 17, the grace note D would coincide with the bass E and the slurred C would follow almost instantaneously.

When there is more than one small note shown before the main note the treatment is the same as for a single grace note; all notes are slurred to the main note, and the first grace note coincides with the beat and hence with the bass note, if there is one. In example (d), from Sor's opus 2, the small E is played with the chord, then the first and second fingers hammer on quickly to sound the F and G.

To play example (e), from Sor's opus 3, the third and first fingers pull off in a single movement and the first finger hammers back to sound the C—all as quickly as possible.

TURNS

A turn consists of four notes that, like the grace note, are invariably slurred. They are played in the order shown in example (f): the auxiliary note above the main note, the main note, the auxiliary note below the main note, and finally the main note again.

When placed between two notes, as in example (g), the main note is played before the turn is begun.

This stylistic distinction is often overlooked by students and, curiously, even by professional performers. The turn on C in example (h), from Giuliani's

Sonata, opus 15, is usually played incorrectly, as if the turn were placed between A and C. It is properly played as shown in example (i).

TRILLS

A trill is a rapid and even alternation of two notes: a main note (the lower) and an auxiliary (the higher). In the simple trill shown in example (j) the main note is B and the auxiliary is C.

In the nineteenth century the trill was conventionally commenced on the main note. The exact number of notes depended upon the tempo and mood of the music. If a special termination was required, it was indicated with small notes, as in example (k). Such small notes were also used to mark an old-style trill that was to be commenced on the auxiliary note, as in example (1).

CADENZAS AND *A PIACERE* PASSAGES

In the grander compositions intended for the concert stage one sometimes finds extended passages in small notes intended as cadenzas, sometimes marked *a piacere* (literally, "as you please"). In these passages the player must exercise his taste, realizing that the composer is giving to the performer a free moment to show his personal musicianship and, at times, virtuosity. The composer of example (m), Giuliani, had just such an intention. In spite of the freedom implied by the marking *a piacere,* such passages should be as fluent and as carefully prepared as those in strict tempo to avoid halting the forward flow of the music.

SFORZANDO

The marking *sforzando* (literally, "forcing") is very common in early classical guitar music, usually abbreviated to *sf* or *sfz*. It means that a sudden strong accent should be given to the note or chord under which it is placed, and in the particular case of the guitar arpeggiation is often used. This may be done with a single sweep of the thumb if the notes are all on adjacent strings, as in the opening chord of example (m).

DOLCE AND SUL PONTICELLO

The indication *dolce* (literally, "sweet") is common in classical scores, and it usually implies a move of the right hand closer to the sound hole to achieve a marked change in tone color. In contrast, the marking *sul ponticello* (literally, "near the bridge") indicates, not surprisingly, a move closer to the bridge, to produce a more crystalline, metallic quality. In later scores the latter term is sometimes replaced by the indication *metallico;* however, both terms are somewhat rare compared to the use of *dolce* or its abbreviation *dol.*

SLIDES

The slide, also known by the Spanish term *arrastre,* is common in late nineteenth-century romantic music. It is used in two ways: as a form of slur and as an ornament similar to a grace note.

In example (o) the slide approximates the sound of the conventional slur in example (n). The F sharp is played and then the left-hand finger slides with a positive movement to the G fret, thereby sounding the G.

In playing example (p) the C is followed immediately by a slide to the fifth fret to sound the E. The right hand does not play the E; the sound comes entirely from left-hand movement. Although very popular in the late nineteenth century, this form of embellishment is today considered somewhat overromantic if it is used to excess.

PORTAMENTO

Portamento involves "carrying" one tone to another by the continuous pressure of the left hand. This has the effect of sounding the intervening tones, not individually but in the form of a continual rise or descent in pitch between the two main notes. The movement should be performed rapidly, since a slow "scoop" from one note to another is musically unacceptable. It should be distinguished from the slide by the fact that both main notes are played by the right hand; the left hand is responsible only for the liaison between them.

In example (q), from Tárrega's *Lagrima,* after the initial chord has been played the second finger of the left hand moves up to the C, maintaining pressure on the fingerboard. The C is then played by the right hand. The apparent grace note should not be taken to imply a double sounding of the C.

TEMPO RUBATO

This term, meaning literally "robbed time," is used most commonly to express the opposite to strict rhythm. Typically the tempo may slow down, hover on a particular note, and then be picked up either in strict tempo or even slightly faster to compensate for the time that has been "robbed." As a general guide, the following points are recommended to all but the most experienced performers.

1. Use rubato with restraint in music prior to the classical period.
2. Confine the slowing of tempo to the *ends* of musical phrases.
3. Commence the following phrase in strict tempo.
4. Do *not* employ this device as an excuse for slowing up at a difficult technical spot; use it only for musically expressive purposes.
5. If in doubt, sing the melody of the passage and decide whether the rubato sounds natural to the voice. If it does not, it is probably not appropriate for the instrument either.

CLASSICAL AND ROMANTIC PERIODS

GENERAL STYLE

The music of both Sor and Giuliani is firmly rooted in the classical style established by Haydn and Mozart. The forms are mostly the simpler ones of the period: divertissements, variations, collections of minuets, rondos, etc. In spite of attempts by both composers the true sonata form for the guitar did not develop, probably because of the difficulties of modulation. Giuliani used the Alberti bass (see lesson four) extensively, Sor less frequently. Sor was interested in multivoiced composition, writing occasionally in four parts but more characteristically in three. Carulli's music, apart from the profusion of simple studies for beginners, was largely programmatic, and some of his more ambitious works contain such "program" instructions as "The Storm Rages," "The Troops Embark," and so on.

Growing romanticism is evident in some works by Matteo Carcassi (1792–1853), more so in those of Sor's friend in later life, Napoleon Coste (1806–1883). But the true genius of romantic music for the guitar was Francisco Tárrega. The influence of Chopin is unmistakable in Tárrega's compositions, and the charm of his miniatures has led many to take up the guitar.

The interpretation of nineteenth-century guitar music contains few mysteries or pitfalls if the composers are considered in their historic context, and if the student takes the time to listen not only to guitar performers playing this music but also to superior instrumentalists of all kinds performing the music that inspired and influenced these composers.

FIVE PIECES WITH STUDY NOTES

STUDY NOTES FOR *DIVERTIMENTO*
by Mauro Giuliani

As the title implies, this is a lighthearted piece intended for diversion. Classified by the composer as

being of "medium difficulty," it should present no problems. It contains some typical configurations that Giuliani used in his grander works, in particular the moving thirds over the repeated open **D**, which acts as a type of pedal point.

DIVERTIMENTO, Op. 40 No. 6   Mauro Giuliani (1781–1829)

STUDY NOTES FOR *ALLEGRO SPIRITOSO*
by Mauro Giuliani

This piece in typical Giuliani style is chosen from the last part of the opus 1 method. The title means "fast and spirited," an effect easy to achieve as the notes lie comfortably under the fingers.

A The fingering here is important: using the third finger on the D releases the second finger for the low G at the beginning of the following measure.

B It may help to practice this passage first as chords, later breaking the thirds when the positions are clear.

ALLEGRO SPIRITOSO, Op. 1 No. 10   Mauro Giuliani (1781–1829)

STUDY NOTES FOR *SICILIANA*
by Fernando Sor

This piece has long been out of print, yet it shares the quality of some of Sor's most celebrated works. One of his later compositions, it demonstrates his thorough knowledge of the fingerboard and his delight in the rich sonorities that can be obtained with the guitar. The chord changes present some challenge, but the tempo is moderate, and there are no problems that are not soluble by extra practice.

$\boxed{A}$ Play both D's with the thumb, taking care not to strike the fourth string.

$\boxed{B}$ Notice that essentially the same chord is being moved to the higher position, and that the fourth, first, and second fingers maintain contact with the strings.

$\boxed{C}$ The third finger remains on the fourth string for this and the following seven measures.

$\boxed{D}$ In the original publication the final cadence is not resolved, since there is an immediate transaction to a rapid march. Because the march is not reprinted here, the cadence has been editorially completed.

SICILIANA, Op. 33 No. 3

Fernando Sor (1778–1839)

STUDY NOTES FOR *PRELUDE IN E*
by Francisco Tárrega

This prelude and the Tárrega mazurka that follows demonstrate in abundance the typical ornamentation of the romantic period. Both pieces are of only moderate difficulty and serve to reinforce note learning in the higher positions.

Tárrega's fingering is, in general, extremely logical, following not always the easiest path but directed to achieving the maximum sonority. The only problems are some stretches that were possible on the smaller nineteenth-century fingerboard but that are too difficult on the modern instrument. Where these occur I have tried to find respectable alternatives, although it is considered almost sacrilegeous to change the maestro's fingering.

A   Note that the B is not played but is sounded by the slide from the F sharp.

B   The small note shows that the F is played by the right hand, so the indication is for *portamento* rather than a slide. There is of course only one F, not a double sound.

PRELUDE IN E   Francisco Tárrega (1852–1909)

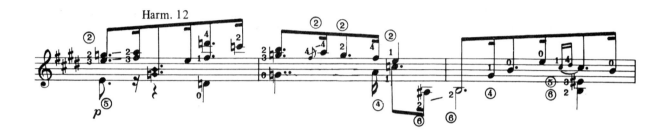

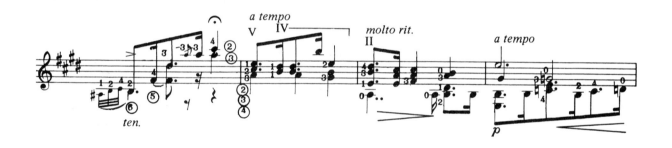

STUDY NOTES FOR *MAZURKA IN G*
by Francisco Tárrega

The mazurka, originally a Polish national dance, was first introduced into serious music by Chopin. In moderate tempo it is characterized by strong accents on the second or third beat of the measure.

[A] The chord with second and fourth fingers is a little awkward, but the original had the whole measure on a third-position bar, which is considerably more difficult.

[B] In this rather curious double slide the fingers must open up as they travel to their respective notes.

[C] This is the type of slide that I believe adds little to the music and might well be omitted. But try it for effect first.

[D] I certainly cannot play this chord while holding the second-position bar, though it may be possible for someone with longer fingers. I believe the best solution is to drop the A sharp, an unimportant change that considerably eases the passage.

MAZURKA IN G

Francisco Tárrega (1852–1909)

LESSON EIGHT
STYLE AND ORNAMENT:
THE LATE RENAISSANCE

IN PERFORMING ANY MUSIC WRITTEN EARLIER THAN the mid-eighteenth century it is of great importance to keep two points in mind. The first is that, because the guitar as we know it today did not then exist, *all* the music, even if nominally written for the guitar, was composed for an instrument with a different sound and different technique advantages or limitations. The second major point is that the music for the plucked stringed instruments was not written in conventional notation but in "tablature," a type of specialized shorthand that showed, by letters or numbers, which fret was to be played.

Thus, all scores available today in conventional notation are in fact transcriptions, and all are influenced to a greater or lesser extent by the point of view of the person who has made the transcription. For instance, amateur guitarists looking for the well-known *Suite in D Minor* by Robert de Visée are frequently confused to find that there are half a dozen versions on the market and that no two of them are exactly alike.

The reason for the different approaches in transcriptions will become apparent from a study of the tablature itself. However, the real issue is whether the music should be played in strict imitation of the early instruments, both with regard to style and to actual sonority, or whether the greater resources of the modern guitar should be exploited to play the early music with more extended dynamic and tonal range than was possible at the time.

The answer for the amateur is, I believe, simple. One need only consider the analogy of the piano. A pianist is most unlikely to exclude from his repertoire the keyboard works of Bach or Scarlatti written originally for the harpsichord. He is equally unlikely to eliminate all dynamics because the harpsichord lacked the capacity for loud and soft playing. So, with the guitar, it seems natural that the amateur would wish to enjoy the early music and to take advantage of the constructional improvements to the instrument that have given it a greater range, without feeling inhibited by those who seek for complete authenticity.

Nevertheless, there *are* points of style that should be observed, just as there are some traps to avoid in playing sixteenth-century music.

TEMPO

Much of the sixteenth-century repertoire was written to accompany dances, the most popular of which were pavans, galliards, and allemands. As in dance music of any period a strict rhythm is essential; the *rallentandos* and *rubato* of the nineteenth century have no place in this music. It is also important to keep a strict tempo relationship between statements of themes and the ornamental repeats that are so typical of the period. Known as "divisions" or "diminutions," these repeats are the principal form of musical decoration of the period.

DIVISIONS

The essential purpose of a division was to ornament a given theme by introducing faster notes. These notes were added not to change the harmony but as skillful embellishments of the melody, which would still remain recognizable. In the early part of the century composers often wrote a song or a dance and followed it with a complete second version with divisions. Later in the century divisions became more common as embellished repeats of one section of a piece.

Since the instrumental embellishment is closely related to that practiced by vocalists, it may be considered first in connection with song. Examples (a) and (b) are two versions of the same song from Luis Milan's *El Maestro,* the first printed collection for an instrument of the guitar family.

In the straightforward version, example (a), Milan's instructions make it clear that the guitarist is to play slowly, allowing the singer to improvise and ornament the melody. In the version with divisions, example (b)—which also constitutes the complete song—it is the turn of the guitarist to create the variety; in this second version the singer is instructed "to sing plain" (*cantar llano*). The second accompaniment is thus a setting of the first with added divisions. Further examples of divisions will be seen in the repertoire section at the end of this lesson.

TRILLS AND RELISHES

During the main part of the period under consideration composers did not include signs or abbreviations for ornaments in the tablatures, but they wrote out all trills in full. Although the exact number of alternated notes varied from one situation to another, the required trill was spelled out exactly, as in example (c).

It is clear also from tablatures containing fingering for the right hand that the trill was performed by rapid alternation of *p* and *i*, thumb and forefinger, not slurred with a left-hand finger. The initial alternating notes were played on a single string, and, as in example (c), the notes forming the termination sometimes involved a string crossing. In general the trill in his period had more the character of a fast division than that of a vocal ornament.

Two curious signs, + and #, appear in the tablature written toward the end of the period. A satisfactory explanation of these symbols has yet to be discovered, and an idea of the complexity of the subject may be afforded by a quotation from Robert Dowland's *Varietie of Lute Lessons* (1610).* In the section entitled "Necessarie Observations Belonging to the Lute" the celebrated Jean-Baptiste Besard wrote: "You should have some rules for the sweet relishes and shakes if they could be expressed here, as they are on the Lute: but seeing they cannot by speech or writing be expressed, thou wert best to imitate some cunning player, or get them by thine own practise, only take heed lest in making too many shakes thou hinder the perfection of the Notes. In sum, if you affect biting sounds, as some call them, which may very well be used, yet use them not in your running, and use them not at all but when you judge them decent."

A likely candidate for the "biting sounds" is the mordent, explained in the discussion of baroque ornamentation in lesson nine, but the term might also refer more generally to the use of quick ornaments involving slurs.

* Facsimile edition published by Schott and Co. Ltd., London, 1958.

In general it seems advisable to treat the "relishes" as the beginning of baroque style, and to play the music of the sixteenth century without extra adornment.

COMMON DANCE FORMS

The Pavan and Galliard

In a steady four beats to the bar, the pavan is usually characterized as "stately" because of its original character as a processional dance. In dance suites it was conventionally followed by the galliard, which afforded a strong contrast of mood by virtue of its lively leaping steps and triple time.

As dances, the two forms were linked in tempo, since the beat was the same or similar for both. However, by the second half of the century each had become a popular instrumental form in its own right, and many pavans were written without an accompanying galliard, and vice versa. The instrumental forms allow perhaps more flexibility in tempo, but the galliard should not be considered as fast so much as lively.

The Alman (Almayn)

Although *alman* (literally, "German") has the same meaning as the baroque *allemand* (see page 133), the terms should be distinguished as names of two rather different dance forms; the earlier dance was lighter in feeling and usually faster in tempo. The almans of the English lute school are usually tuneful and cheerful in nature, and although they retain their dance character they include a number of well-developed instrumental solos.

The Coranto

A popular, short dance in brisk tempo, the coranto contained running steps and was light-hearted in nature. There are a few extended pieces written specifically for instrumental playing, but the coranto remained predominantly a dance form throughout the period, together with the exuberant volt and the lively gigue.

THE FANTASIA

The most important nondance form, the fantasia was a purely instrumental piece in contrapuntal form developed during the course of the sixteenth century to a level of sophistication approaching that of the fugue. Although a detailed analysis of the form is beyond the scope of this book, advanced players will find some of the most interesting and challenging works of the period under this title.

FIVE PIECES WITH STUDY NOTES

Some representative pieces of the sixteenth century are presented on the following pages. A further collection from this period is contained in my book *The Renaissance Guitar* (New York: Ariel Music Publications, 1974).

STUDY NOTES FOR *PAVAN,*
"THE EARL OF SALISBURY,"
by William Byrd

This is perhaps the best-known pavan by the leading composer of the English school of the late
Renaissance. Although the original was for the
keyboard, the transcription has historical precedent
in a number of lute tablatures of the time arranged
from Byrd's keyboard works.

In pavans written for the lute it is more common to find, instead of a simple repeat, elaborate
written divisions following each segment.

A   The fingering is somewhat contrived here, but
it is the only practical solution.

PAVAN, "THE EARL OF SALISBURY"

William Byrd (c. 1542–1643)

STUDY NOTES FOR *GALLIARD,* "*HEIGH HO HOLIDAY,*"
by Anthony Holborne

Holborne was one of the principal lute composers of the Elizabethan period, and the dedicatee of John Dowland's *Second Book of Songs or Ayres.* He was particularly inventive in both his harmonies and rhythms and, like many of the keyboard composers, favored *hemiola* rhythm, illustrated in

this piece by the abrupt change from 6/8 to 3/4 in the third and second measures from the end of the piece.

A The sudden extra speed here requires practice so as not to slow down the overall tempo.

B The change to 6/8 should be made clear by accentuation of the first and fourth beats.

C Accenting each of the three beats heightens the contrast with the preceding 6/8 measures.

GALLIARD, "HEIGH HO HOLIDAY"

Anthony Holborne (fl. late 1500s)

STUDY NOTES FOR *GALLIARD*
by Francis Cutting

This piece shows the typical form of the English galliard: each of three eight-bar sections is followed by a repeat with divisions. For the sake of clarity all six sections are ended with double bars.

For a piece almost entirely in the first and second positions, it will be found to be remarkably ingenious in construction and full of variety and interest.

[A] The half note E should be accentuated to show the beginning of the bass sequence, and this may be carried with the A and D occupying the same position in the two following measures.

[B] Sufficient accent should be given to sustain the notes of the middle voice and bring out the sequence.

[C] In this repeat section the same accentuation should be given to bring out the middle voice; the situation here is the same as at [B].

GALLIARD

Francis Cutting (fl. late 1500s)

STUDY NOTES FOR *ALMAN,*
"HIT AND TAKE IT,"
by Robert Johnson

Johnson's music is characterized by a strong sense of melody and a gift for simple but effective counterpoint. The alman "Hit and Take It," justly a favorite among lutenists, transcribes easily to the guitar.

A This is the one trouble spot in an otherwise straightforward piece. Care must be taken to place the fourth finger in a good position on the high C, i.e., on its tip and not stretched out straight. After playing the preceding B the hand must be moved to accommodate this— then the bass notes will lie comfortably under the first and third fingers.

B Lift the bass end of the bar slightly to play the open A.

ALMAN, "HIT AND TAKE IT"

Robert Johnson (1583–1633)

STUDY NOTES FOR *FANTASIA*
by Francesco da Milano

This fantasia, a typical work by one of the most celebrated composers of the first half of the sixteenth century, introduces special tuning whereby the third string is tuned down a half-step to F

sharp. This makes the relationship of the strings the same as that on the lute, with the result that lute music may be played with great ease while maintaining the open strings. Many guitarists object to this D tuning, but it is really no more difficult to handle than the very common tuning of the bottom string to D.

FANTASIA

Francesco da Milano (1497–1543)

LESSON NINE
STYLE AND ORNAMENT:
THE BAROQUE PERIOD

STUDENTS TEND TO APPROACH BAROQUE MUSIC with greater trepidation than that of any other period, fearing that their attempts at interpretation will lead them to reveal ignorance and to commit solecisms inexcusable to the knowledgeable. The reason is to be found in the current revival of interest in preclassical music, which has involved rejecting the haphazard and romantic approach of the late nineteenth century in favor of a more authentic approach, based on the instructions of the composers themselves and other contemporary writings.

Although much genuine understanding has emerged from this revival, so has much specious academicism. The first wave of enthusiasts tended to be pedantic and unyielding in their opinions, giving rise to heated controversy and a surfeit of pettifoggery. The result of this was that fine musical performances were often dismissed by the new cognoscenti on some technical ground, more often than not based on the execution of ornaments.

Today a calmer approach reigns with the passing of what Louis Crowder has called "the panic period of Baroque interpretation," * and we find with relief that Bach need not, or should not, be played with the regularity of a sewing machine. In addition, guitarists have found that there is a difference between keyboard and fingerboard ornamentation. The latter, which is confined to comparatively few conventional signs, is simpler.

Perhaps the most important point to keep in mind about the ornaments is that many of them commenced on a dissonant note, reflecting a move away from the strict rules of the Renaissance. These moments of dissonance add a certain spice to the music beyond the realm of mere decoration, and the removal of them by nineteenth-century editors on grounds of taste led to much of the misunderstanding that remains today.

The characteristic ornaments may be more easily understood by the guitarist than the keyboard player, since almost all of them are simple varieties of the slur.

* See Crowder's introduction to Denes Agay's piano anthology, *The Baroque Period* (New York: Yorktown Music Press, 1971).

MORDENTS

The mordent, for instance, is nothing more than a pull-off followed by a hammer, both executed as quickly as possible consistent with clarity.

The word derives from the Italian *mordere,* "to bite," and is particularly expressive in the case of plucked strings. In example (a) the time value given is only approximate; speed and clarity are the important elements.

SHAKES (PASSING TRILLS)

The mordent ends with a hammer stroke. If to this is added an immediate additional pull-off the ornament becomes a shake, or passing trill.

The shake commences on the note *above* the main note, which bears the shorthand ornament sign, except in the case of a descending scale.

In example (c) notice that although the F is not repeated, as this would interrupt the downward flow of the scale, it still in a sense commences the movement, since after it is sounded the remaining notes are slurred to it.

As in the example of the mordent, the note values are only approximate. However the ornaments must never slow down the regular tempo of the music, and thus should be practiced individually until the necessary rapidity is achieved.

CADENTIAL TRILLS

During the baroque period the longer trills associated with final cadences remained in substantially the same form as those of the late Renaissance, but the execution was changed by the use of the slur. Thus the trill came to resemble an ornament as much as a division.

Example (d) shows the most common form of cadential trill. Although the alternating C and B are slurred, they should be played with regularity rather than with the fast-as-you-can approach needed for the smaller embellishments. The alternating C and B must be slurred, but the final A and B may or may not be, according to fingerboard convenience.

Modern editors tend to give somewhat fuller indications of the required trill, and most would write the above as shown in example (e).

There are many variants of the common form of cadential trill quoted above, and the three most typical to the guitar are given in example (f). The elaborate shorthand signs of the later baroque period are not used in guitar music and are therefore not listed.

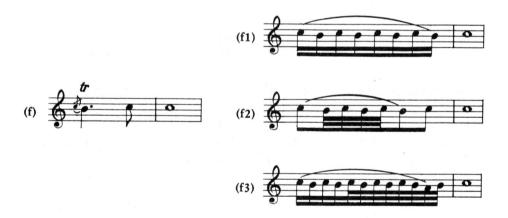

In example (f1) the termination of the common trill is eliminated, resulting in a simple alternation of two notes. In example (f2) variety is achieved by lengthening the initial dissonant note, thereby giving it more prominence. In example (f3) the initial tempo of the trill is doubled, again for variety; this form is suitable when the tempo is very slow.

APPOGGIATURAS

The appoggiatura (Italian, *appoggiare*, "to lean") consists of a simple slur between two notes, the first more stressed than the second so that it "leans" on it. In abbreviated form the first note is the smaller, and—whether or not a slur is marked—it must always be slurred to the main note.

The following examples show the most common use of the abbreviation in transcriptions intended for the guitar.

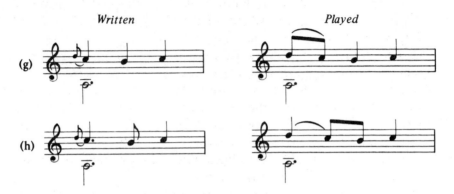

In example (g) the appoggiatura "borrows" half the value of the following note. In example (h), where the dotted note is not divisible in two, the appoggiatura occupies two-thirds of the value of the following note.

It should be understood that the exact length of the appoggiatura varied considerably during the baroque period and that the variants of this ornament involve a considerable separate study beyond the scope of this book. The interpretation given is the intention in the vast majority of scores that will be encountered by the guitarist and is therefore sufficient for practical purposes.

The stylistic significance of the appoggiatura is that a nonharmonic or dissonant tone bears an accent, and it thus represents a departure from Renaissance tradition. It should be carefully distinguished from the grace note of the classical period (see lesson seven), which has a similar appearance but a totally different character.

IMPROVISED ORNAMENTS

In preclassical music, free ornamentation by the instrumentalist or singer was common, and—although progress toward the codification and classification of specific ornaments can be seen throughout the period—every performer had his own armory of "sweet relishes and shakes" to be used at his own discretion. Typical of such varieties, rarely notated, are the whole fall, the single relish, the double relish, and others explained by Thomas Mace in his *Musicks Monument* (London, 1676).* The guitarist interested in experimenting in this area should concentrate first on acquiring a real

* Facsimile edition published by Centre National de la Recherche Scientifique, Paris, 1966.

period sense. The variety of fine recordings available today makes it possible to hear the best interpreters, and there is an abundance of literature on the subject. Particularly recommended is Robert Donington's *The Interpretation of Early Music,* new version (New York: St. Martin's Press, 1974), which contains an extensive bibliography.

THE BAROQUE SUITE

By far the greatest proportion of music for the guitar and lute composed during the baroque period is made up of the formalized dances that were grouped together in a certain order and called a suite.

The main components of the suite were, in order and by their French names, the *allemande,* the *courante,* the *sarabande,* and the *gigue.* To these central elements were added many optional dances; the commonest in the guitar and lute literature were the *bourrée,* the *menuet,* the *gavotte,* and the *passacaille.* The suites of the two best-known guitar composers, Robert de Visée and Francesco Corbetta, were usually organized with the optional dances following the gigue, but J. S. Bach customarily included them after the saraband, saving the fast-moving gigue as a finale.

The main elements of the suite are characterized below, with the caution that considerable differences in style occurred not only between nationalities but also between individual composers of the same nation as the suite moved through stages of evolution.

The Prelude

The prelude is free in style and is the only nondance composition connected with the suite. For this reason it is not usually considered a part of the suite so much as an introduction to it. For the plucked instruments the prelude afforded the opportunity to loosen the fingers and check the tuning. Preludes often had no bar lines and contained chords that were to be freely arpeggiated.

The Allemand

In stately, moderate tempo, the allemand was customarily in 4/4 time commencing with a short upbeat. As with all the main dances, the structure was in two parts, each repeated, with the first half ending in the dominant key and the second with a return to the tonic. Any inclination to play an allemand fast should be resisted, as this spoils the contrast of mood and tempo with the following movement.

The Courant

In marked contrast to the four-square rhythm of the allemand, the French-style courant in mixed 3/2 and 6/4 time was lively in spirit, although not fast in tempo. The shift in stress from a beat of three to that of two triplets added interest and occasional ambiguity to the rhythm, which makes the courant somewhat harder for the amateur to phrase at first reading. The

Italian form, the *corrente,* was simpler in structure, consisting of a flowing, brisk-moving melody in three time.

The Saraband

In marked contrast to its earlier character, the middle and late baroque saraband was slow in tempo, embodying both grandeur and intensity. The sarabands of J. S. Bach in particular exhibited an emotional intensity not shared by any of the other dances, characterized often by a sense of high tension alternated with release. In general the saraband was the grand, slow movement of the suite.

The Gigue

The gigue was a fast-moving lively dance, usually in 6/8 time, which eventually became the usual finale to the suite. The French form, with separate voices and imitations, does not lend itself to quite the presto tempo appropriate to the Italian variety, which for the guitar and lute usually involved two parts only, with the interest in the melody. Sprightly, strict in tempo, and light in mood, the gigue may be considered the antithesis to the saraband.

Optional Dances

In contrast to the main members of the suite, which had lost their close association with the dance, the optional group included such modern popular dances as the minuet, the bourrée, and the gavot. The less sophisticated "pop" element of these dances may be preserved by maintaining a strong sense of the rhythms and by visualizing groups of dancers enjoying a ball.

Less popular in the ballroom were the chaconne and the passacaille, French versions of dances from Spain and Italy. They were, however, popular with the guitar composers, perhaps because they afforded the opportunity for ingenuity without the problems of modulation. Both consisted of a series of variations on a fixed bass or harmonic structure, and in the French form the original statement, known as a couplet, was repeated after each variation.

SEVEN PIECES WITH STUDY NOTES

The repertoire offered here will give a practical opportunity for the study of the components of the baroque suite. Works by several composers have been chosen to illustrate variety of approach. For further selections from this period, see my book *The Baroque Guitar* (New York: Ariel Music Publications, 1974).

STUDY NOTES FOR *PRELUDE*
by G. F. Handel

This simple prelude is from a suite written for a musical clock, a form of musical box whose mechanical movement represented the only means at the time of "recording" music. Naturally the range is limited, but in spite of this the "broken style" of arpeggios gives the impression of a fuller range of harmony. The tempo of a prelude is quite free, and the metronome marking should be taken as a suggestion only.

PRELUDE

G. F. Handel (1685–1759)

STUDY NOTES FOR *ALLEMAND*
by J. S. Bach

The famous *Suite in E minor,* BWV 996, is usually assumed to be intended for the lute from its texture and resemblance to other lute compositions by Bach. Unfortunately, no autograph manuscript remains to give final authority to the supposition.

This allemand, which transcribes well to the guitar, should present no undue difficulty.

A | The jump of the second finger from the E to the B requires practice. Try to avoid giving short value to the E.

B | The placement of the fourth finger on the F sharp requires care.

C | The movement of the third finger up to the high B must be carefully practiced.

D | A slight emphasis on the open B and the fourth-finger F sharp gives attention to the upper voice and helps to balance this passage.

ALLEMAND   J. S. Bach (1685–1750)

COURANT

Robert de Visée (1660–1720)

STUDY NOTES FOR *COURANT* AND *GAVOT*
by Robert de Visée

These two de Visée pieces can be used to supplement the selection from the **D** minor suite presented in Book 1. The courant has the typical irregular and often ambiguous rhythm of the French style.

The suggested ornamentation in the courant, although simple, adds much to the piece if exe-cuted with precision and neatness. In the gavot the ornaments are not written out but should be executed like those in the courant.

[A] The C may legitimately be shortened to a sixteenth note to give the effect of double dotting in this passage and the similar sequences that follow. This is the type of refinement that helps to give a truly baroque feeling to a piece of this kind.

GAVOT

Robert de Visée (1660–1720)

STUDY NOTES FOR *SARABAND*
by S. L. Weiss

The music of Weiss has for many years suffered total neglect, since it existed only in tablature for the baroque lute and in manuscript form. Nevertheless, he was a fine composer, respected by J. S. Bach and the other leading musicians of his time, and thanks to modern transcriptions his works are now being revived, in particular by guitarists.

The saraband has a serious, brooding character that calls for a very moderate tempo and a sustained quality throughout.

Because of the slower tempo, the trills should be more extended. There is considerable scope for experimentation here.

A The stretch seems too much at first but is possible if the hand is opened up.
B The move to the second string is necessary to prepare for the chord that follows.
C Drop the first finger into half-bar position while keeping contact with the E flat.

SARABAND

S. L. Weiss (1686–1748)

STUDY NOTES FOR *GIGUE*
by Lodovico Roncalli

The guitar works of Roncalli, an Italian count, are contemporaneous with those of de Visée, but they show a very different character and much individuality. The music is simple but strong in melody, exhibiting an unsophisticated charm. This gigue is easy enough to play at a very lively tempo, which is necessary for the music to be effective.

[A] The move to fifth position is sudden and requires some extra practice so that the rhythm is not lost here.

GIGUE

Lodovico Roncalli (fl. late 1600s)

STUDY NOTES FOR *FANTASIA*
by S. L. Weiss

The first section of this work is, in fact, an un-measured prelude. This broad, arpeggiated structure in free form, so typical to baroque music for the lute, leads to and contrasts with the fuguelike second section, which requires a more formal approach and strict rhythm.

[A] Care must be taken to avoid undue "snap" in the slurs on the first string. This passage is not easy and requires practice.

[B] The extended section on the seventh-position bar is tiring to practice but passes quickly enough when the piece is played up to time. Sufficient emphasis should be given to the bass so that the B pedal point will sustain.

[C] This is a problem spot, because of the necessity of reaching back with the third finger to the sixth string. However, it is possible with careful practice.

[D] At this point the F sharp is played by the first finger at the point where it normally bars; the rest of the finger is stretched out ready to drop onto the second-position bar that follows. This seemingly strange technique is not difficult and is most useful in situations such as this.

[E] Arpeggios were not always written out by composers of this period; the arpeggiation was left to the player to interpret from simple chord indications. Following the lead of Julian Bream, many players use the formula illustrated below for this passage.

FANTASIA   S. L. Weiss (1686–1748)

LESSON TEN
TWO CONCERT MASTERPIECES

AT THE CONCLUSION OF THE SECOND EDITION of Book 1 a number of pieces are presented that are more technically challenging than the repertoire in the body of the book, on the theory that these might represent a goal and an incentive to do the necessary preparatory study. Following the same principle, the present course concludes with two pieces that have been delighting concert audiences for the past half century.

These pieces are among Francisco Tárrega's finest works. Neither involves any specific technique that has not already been studied in detail, and both maintain a similar right-hand pattern throughout. The reason these works are considered more advanced is that they require a certain endurance that relates both to the muscular preparation of the hands and to the continuous level of concentration. In addition, a longer period of time is normally required to attain the necessary smoothness than would be allocated to the majority of pieces; i.e., when memorization is complete and the piece thoroughly learned, a period of months may profitably be given to further detailing and refinement.

In spite of the considerable work involved, teachers have long recognized the didactic value of both studies, understanding also that the magnetic attraction of the music provides both incentive and reward.

RECUERDOS DE LA ALHAMBRA

This original composition is a musical memory of the famous Alhambra palace in Granada, a magnificent relic of the splendor and grace of court life during the Moorish occupation of Spain. The rippling tremolo melody is evocative of the fountains and running water that are to be found everywhere in the palace and its gardens.

The basic principles of the tremolo are covered in Book 1, but a few reminders are appropriate before commencing the piece.

1. First practice the tremolo with simple left-hand chords, so that the concentration can be focused on the right hand.
2. Start slowly, but remember that the particular effect of tremolo depends upon speed, which must be the final objective. The metronome can be used as with the scales.

Exercise 42

3. Exercise 42 is a particularly useful preparation. After working the speed up in this pattern, relax the hand and play the normal tremolo, which will be found to be much improved in most cases.

4. When playing the tremolo on the second string, be particularly careful to keep the *a* finger close to the string, to avoid accidentally striking the first string. The fingers must be close together and the movement minimized.

5. Do not neglect the thumb, which is as important as the fingers in balancing the tremolo. The thumb stroke must *not* move the hand, which should remain in a fixed position. However, the thumb must play strongly enough to give a clear accompaniment to the melody.

ESTUDIO BRILLANTE

This famous piece is an adaptation of a violin étude by the celebrated nineteenth-century virtuoso Delfin Alard. The style is reminiscent of the piano études of Chopin, particularly the *Allegro Sostenuto in A flat,* op. 25. The piece exploits to the full the particular magic of a well-executed arpeggio on the guitar, out of which emerges, seemingly from a second instrument, a romantically attractive melody. As with the tremolo, the particular effect is dependent upon a certain speed, which must be the final objective.

The Right Hand

Example (a) shows the basic pattern and fingering for the right hand, which should be thoroughly practiced before commencing. The melody notes, played by the *a* finger of the right hand, should be executed with a light rest stroke. This must not throw the hand off position, and in this balance between the rest stroke of the melody and the free stroke of the remainder of the arpeggio lies the key to this study.

Undoubtedly, it will be argued that the piece can be played with free stroke throughout, since with good control the *a*-finger stroke can be accented to bring out the melody. But it is much harder this way to produce the effect of two instruments, which, to my ear at least, is a large part of the effectiveness of the piece.

The Left Hand

In both pieces particular attention should be given to correct placement of the full bar without more pressure than is necessary. Otherwise the hand will tire, and continued practice becomes impossible. The important reminder is that a correctly placed bar does not take much strength; it is the extra pressure put on to correct a poor position that causes fatigue.

The frequent movements covering the entire fingerboard necessitate a good left hand and arm position throughout; care should be taken to avoid lifting the left elbow when traveling from a high to a low position. As endurance is involved, the lightest touch consistent with a clear note will be found to be the most effective.

STUDY NOTES FOR
RECUERDOS DE LA ALHAMBRA
by Francisco Tárrega

[A] When reaching back for the seventh-position bar leave the third finger firmly on the C.

[B] The triplets are important to the piece and should receive detailed practice.

[C] The reason for the cross-fingering with the fourth finger is that it is much easier to slide the second and third fingers down as a chord following the triplet.

[D] The unconventional fingering in this measure is directed toward easing the move to the first-position bar.

[E] At this point the first finger must cover the C and the G sharp. After the triplet the side of the finger lifts to clear the open string.

[F] It is a good idea to take the complete chord up from the second position leaving the second finger on as well. It is then ready for the move back.

[G] The repeats may be simply explained as follows: The first time bar is a link to a repeat of the A major section. Following that, the second time bar leads back to the beginning of the piece, which is played through ignoring any other repeats up to the third time bar, which leads to the coda that concludes the piece.

RECUERDOS DE LA ALHAMBRA

Francisco Tárrega (1852–1909)

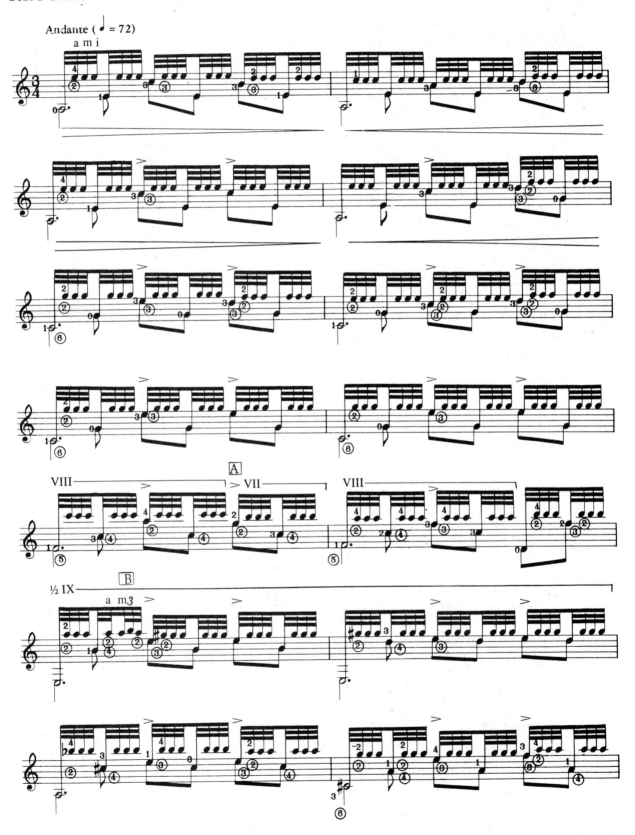

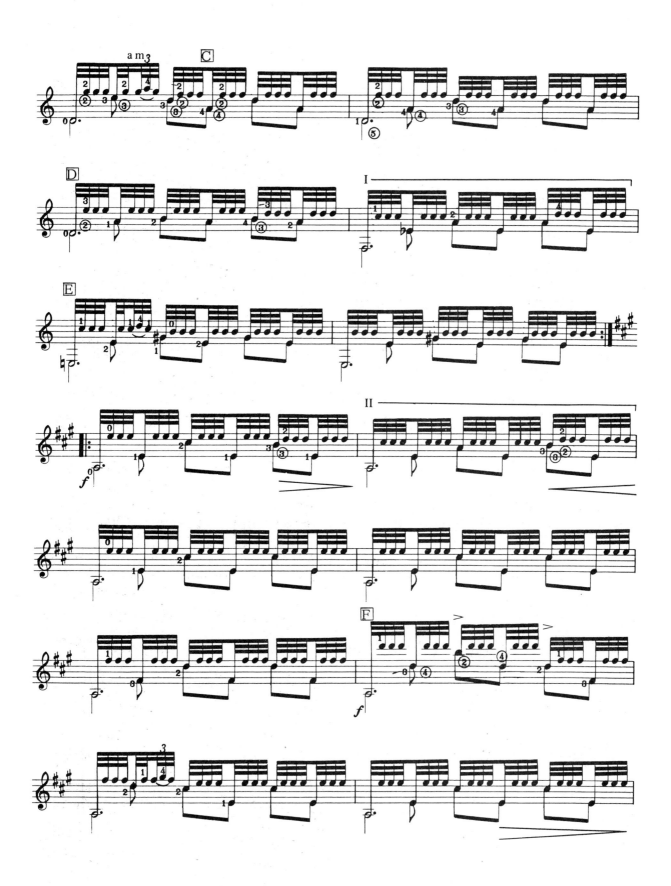

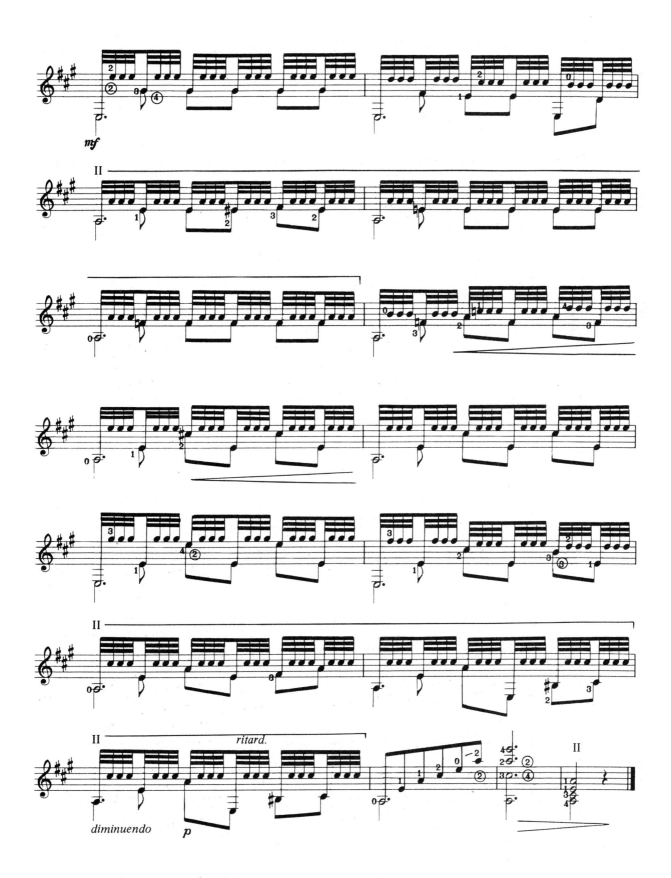

STUDY NOTES FOR
ESTUDIO BRILLANTE DE ALARD
by Francisco Tárrega

[A] The original calls for a second-position bar here, with the D taken by the fourth finger. This enables the D to be sustained but presents extreme difficulty.

[B] The original has a seventh-position bar for the complete measure, awkward on the modern fingerboard.

[C] The original used the second string from the B onward. I believe it is easier to keep the logical order of strings.

[D] Some of the best players favor the modification shown below.

[E] The slur between D and C sharp and the right-hand fingering are editorial and, I believe, help considerably to maintain the tempo through this difficult run. Players who object to the repeated *i* finger may substitute *a*, but I personally believe that, because of the intervening slur, the repeat is unobjectionable.

[F] In spite of the grace note, the second and third fingers should go on together as a chord. The A bass was a half note in the original, here corrected to a quarter note as it is impossible to sustain.

ESTUDIO BRILLANTE DE ALARD   Francisco Tárrega (1852–1909)

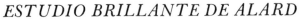

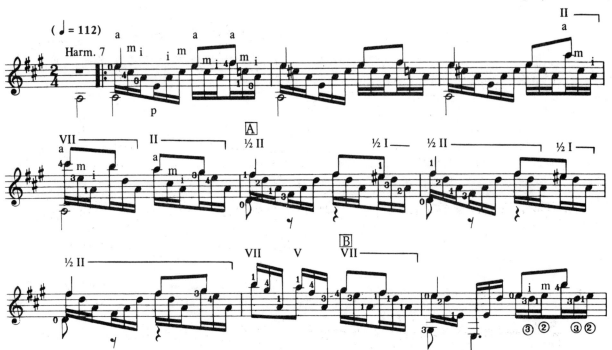